IMAGES
of America

DETROIT'S STATLER AND BOOK-CADILLAC HOTELS

THE ANCHORS OF WASHINGTON BOULEVARD

D1451900

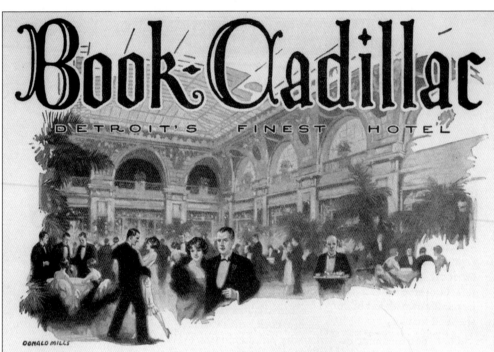

Book·Cadillac

DETROIT'S FINEST HOTEL

DONALD MILLS

"And the nights shall be filled with music"

Colored with romance, a tall spire, filled with pleasant things, with music, with banqueters, with laughter, the Book-Cadillac gathers its youth and its wisdom from 'round the world. From 'round the world, from its further obscure hamlets and from its capitals come these changing, interesting, aggressive folk who people the "Book." In the Blue Room, in the Venetian Room and in the Italian Garden there's always a pageant. Nights *are* filled with music. Cares *can* be forgotten. Yet, *your* room, *all* of the sleeping rooms are quiet, for they are above the seventh floor, and the music and revelry are far below. The beds are soft, famously soft and restful and comfortable. Store that deep in your memory ٧٧٧ Many come here now and often, and they feel at home, for this place knows them well, and they know it. As we've welcomed them so we welcome you. We'll do our best to make your visit memorable, unforgettable. Men say that it is one of America's great hotels.

THE BOOK-CADILLAC HOTEL COMPANY, DETROIT
Roy Carruthers, *President*

THIS you'll like because it protects your family: As you leave, you'll find attached to your receipted bill *an accident insurance policy.* For forty-eight hours from that minute, it guards you and your family; an extension of Book-Cadillac service. It pays $5,000.00 for accidental death; $2,500.00 for loss of limb; and $25.00 weekly over a long term for wholly disabling injuries.

"AND THE NIGHTS SHALL BE FILLED WITH MUSIC." The wonders and services of Detroit's newest and largest hotel are described with elegant detail in this mid-1920s advertisement. (Courtesy Matthew Furman.)

IMAGES
of America

DETROIT'S STATLER AND BOOK-CADILLAC HOTELS

THE ANCHORS OF WASHINGTON BOULEVARD

David Kohrman

ARCADIA

Published by Arcadia Publishing,
an imprint of Tempus Publishing, Inc.
3047 N. Lincoln Ave., Suite 410
Chicago, IL 60657

Printed in Great Britain.

Library of Congress Catalog Card Number: 2002109311

For all general information contact Arcadia Publishing at:
Telephone 843-853-2070
Fax 843-853-0044
E-Mail sales@arcadiapublishing.com

For customer service and orders:
Toll-Free 1-888-313-2665

Visit us on the internet at http://www.arcadiapublishing.com

AN ELEGANT THOROUGHFARE. The Book-Cadillac Hotel dominates this early picture postcard of Washington Boulevard.

CONTENTS

ACKNOWLEDGMENTS

Obtaining interesting photographs was crucial to the success of this project. Therefore I am indebted to everyone who provided assistance with my hunt. Matthew Furman was kind enough to make several historic images from his collection available. Dan Kosmowski is a talented photographer who allowed me to use his amazing contemporary photographs of these buildings. Nancy Bowman not only lent photographs, she also provided information about living in the Statler during her youth, and of her father, its manager. Dawn Eurich of the Burton Historical Collection, Alyn Thomas of Manning Brothers, and Mary Wallace of the Walter Reuther Library were a great help in assisting me find and publish many of the wonderful images from these historic collections.

There are a number of other people without whom this project would not have been possible. Thus to them many thanks are due. I thank Lucas McGrail, Dan Kosmowski (again), C.J. Miller, and Josh Kahl. Tim Trower's advice and information has helped me greatly in my study of the wonderful Statler organization. Thanks also to Brendan McKenna and Maura Brown of Arcadia Publishing, the faculty and students of Western Michigan University's History Department, and to my family for putting up with me.

INTRODUCTION

Hotels have long played an important economic, social, and civic role to the American city. Any city aspiring for greatness had to have at least one first-rate hotel. During the first half of the 20th century, Detroit was blessed with two such elegant institutions. Thousands flocked to them daily. Their restaurants, ballrooms, and bars became the most popular places to spend an evening. Their massive meeting rooms served Detroit civic and industrial leaders. To some, the Statler and Book-Cadillac *were* downtown Detroit.

In some regards, the Statler and Book-Cadillac had little in common. The Statler was the product of a far-off corporation that had developed every aspect of the hotel industry into a science. The Book-Cadillac, by contrast, came from an architect with no hotel experience and was funded by local developers motivated by a vision for Detroit.

Still, in many ways their stories are alike. They were both born amid "Dynamic Detroit's" pre-Depression boom. Both hotels would enjoy 60-year runs. Both were the haunts of presidents, royalty, and celebrities. Both hotels represented technological innovation: the Statler featured private baths and air conditioning; the Book-Cadillac claimed a rooftop radio station. The two fell to the big hotel chains of the post-World War II era. The most unfortunate similarity was that both suffered long, humiliating declines. By the time these hotels were shuttered, they had become merely tattered versions of their past selves. They both stand today as empty buildings, problems for Detroit's image and development.

The pages and photographs that follow are an attempt to look back at the glory years of the Statler and Book-Cadillac. This book begins with background on the explosive growth of Detroit along Washington Boulevard. The bulk of the pages detail the hotels in their prime, from each hotel's debut to just after the Second World War. The conclusion details their decline and vacancy. A new chapter for each hotel is about to start, be it their destruction or revival. I hope you enjoy this look back at both their and Detroit's history.

One

THE FIFTH AVENUE
OF THE MIDWEST

ON THE EVE OF CHANGE. At the beginning of the 20th century, much of Washington Boulevard looked like this view from Grand Circus Park. During the Gilded Age, many prominent Detroiters, such as tobacconist and former governor John J. Bagley, built their homes here. By the early 1900s, most of the residences were replaced with bars and lumberyards. However, as Detroit blossomed into the new century, the central business district began a northward migration. When this photograph was taken in 1911, visionaries were already picturing the Boulevard as a major center of commerce. This would be the backdrop for two of the greatest hotels in the world. (Burton Historical Collection.)

THE CADILLAC HOTEL. Washington Boulevard's intersection with Michigan Avenue already had a history as a site for fine hotels. Tobacco tycoon Daniel Scotten's Cadillac Hotel of 1888 was the third such enterprise on the site. Boasting 200 rooms, the Cadillac was typical of the high-class hotels of its day. It was here that Dr. and Mrs. James Book raised their three sons. These three brothers, James Burgess, Frank Palms, and Herbert Vivian, would grow up to play a primary role in the dramatic transformation of their former childhood home. (Burton Historical Collection.)

THE PONTCHARTRAIN HOTEL. The old Cadillac was a nice hotel for its day, but Detroit's leading hotel and social center in the years immediately prior to the First World War was the Pontchartrain. Built in 1907, it stood over Cadillac Square, then the center of town. The hotel's bars soon became a meeting place for automobile industry executives. However, the Pontchartrain an obsolete structure, lacking private baths and other services that guests would soon expect. It lasted only until 1920. (Author's Collection.)

THE TULLER. Lew Tuller's hotel on Grand Circus Park fared better than its rivals. Its location on the park, just a block from Washington Boulevard, proved advantageous as the area blossomed. The hotel first opened in 1906, but later expansions resulted in an eclectic-looking structure. The Tuller's popularity peaked with the Roaring Twenties.

11

AN EARLY VISION. This graphic, published in 1912, illustrates an early vision for Washington Boulevard's future. Using an actual photograph for comparison, a street lined with uniform low-rise business blocks is shown. The boulevard itself has been replaced with an unusual traffic set-up. Pedestrians enjoy wide sidewalks and bridges, while cars race by below. Absent in this scheme were the two hotels and other high-rises that would play an important role in the boulevard's actual growth. (Burton Historical Collection.)

MAKE WAY FOR PROGRESS. By 1912, some of what was predicted in the illustration began to take shape. Here we see a group of old homes on their way out. The site would soon be home to the Washington Theater. Within a year, the Statler Hotel would take shape to the north. (Burton Historical Collection.)

THE FIFTH AVENUE OF THE MIDWEST. Twelve years after the previous vision was published, Detroiters were given this view of a future Washington Boulevard. Produced by architect Lewis Kamper for the Book brothers, several soaring towers line the length of a landscaped street. A massive hotel anchors each end.

DETROIT'S BEST SELLERS. That is how the three Book brothers were described in the twenties. James, Frank, and Herbert inherited a large fortune, including a vast holding of property along Washington Boulevard, from their father in 1916. The three used this inheritance to pursue the dream of shaping Washington Boulevard into the "Fifth Avenue of the Midwest." They planned 10 skyscrapers, apartments, office buildings, and a grand hotel. The purchase of the old Cadillac Hotel in 1917 made the latter possible.

THE BOOK BUILDING. The first component of the Books' vision was the 13-story Book Building of 1917. Architect Lewis Kamper was hired to design the Italian building. The Books were fully impressed and went on to hire Kamper for all of their future projects. (Burton Historical Collection.)

BOOK TOWER. In 1926, the Books completed what was to be their tallest building. The 36-story Book Tower was an extension of the older Book Building. With its copper roof, this highly detailed Italian Renaissance tower proved an excellent match for the Book-Cadillac Hotel. Yet, even this tower was not the limit of the Books' ambition. (Burton Historical Collection.)

WASHINGTON BOULEVARD IN 1929. The stock market crash of October 1929 effectively killed the remaining projects that would have completed the Books' original vision. This view from Grand Circus Park shows the street as it appeared for much of the 20th century. There are a few less skyscrapers than planned, but the street is now clearly a major commercial and social center. (Burton Historical Collection.)

AN UNREALIZED MONSTER. One project that never survived the Great Depression was the second Book Tower. Planned to have 81 floors and loom 823 feet over the street, it would have been the tallest building in the world.

PICTURE POSTCARD. Even without an 81-story tower, the Boulevard was an attractive subject for popular picture postcards. In this card from the 1920s, the Book-Cadillac and Statler Hotels figure prominently.

18

THE BOULEVARD IN 1980. By the late 1970s, new construction again began to change the look of the street. Building plans attempted to fill in some of the gaps left in the wake of the Great Depression. The greatest change was the removal of one side of traffic and its replacement with a park-like setting. This photograph was taken at the time of the 1980 Republican National Convention. The Statler was already closed, and the Book-Cadillac would soon follow. (Burton Historical Collection.)

THE BOULEVARD IN 2002. Little has changed in 12 years. Most of the buildings from the Boulevard's expansion in the 1920s remain intact. However, two of the street's most important buildings have been vacant since the mid-1970s and 1980s. Let us now look more closely at these landmarks.

Two

THE STATLER HOTEL
1915–1975

"THE COMPLETE HOTEL." The Statler Hotel dominates the northern end of Washington Boulevard. Part of a revolutionary chain of hotels, this was the first hotel in Detroit to have a private bath in every room, as well as the first hotel in the nation to have air conditioning. With a 60-year run, the Statler would establish itself as an integral part of Detroit and set the standard for any competitor. (Manning Brothers Historic Photographic Collection.)

E.M. STATLER. E.M. Statler entered the hotel industry as a bellboy when he was only 13 years old. He quickly proved himself a hard and capable worker and worked his way up, eventually managing a profitable restaurant in Buffalo and two temporary hotels at the Buffalo and St. Louis World's Fairs. Filled with remarkable ideas of what a hotel should be, in 1907 he set out to change the industry.

THE BUFFALO STATLER. It seems remarkable that this building is one of the most important built in the 20th century. The first Statler Hotel opened in Buffalo in 1907. Statler startled the industry by providing unheard-of amenities like a private bathroom for every guestroom, circulating ice water, and closets. Initially mocked, the hotel's success spoke for itself. (Courtesy Matthew Furman.)

22

The LOBBY

The GRILL ROOM

THE CLEVELAND STATLER. With Statler's second hotel in 1912, he was given the opportunity to improve upon his previous design, especially its aesthetics. Statler hired architect George P. Post to design the new hotel and Louis Rorimer to decorate it. This team created a 700-room Italian showplace. Greater construction cost would pay off as the Cleveland Statler became even more esteemed than its predecessor. With fine decor, multiple restaurants, and large ballrooms, the new Statler would be the model for all first-rate hotels of the next 30 years. Post and Rorimer became Statler's team for future projects, including the Detroit Statler. (Burton Historical Collection.)

THE BOSTON STATLER. Using the same designers for each hotel eventually generated criticism that his hotels were too much alike. However, Statler's last hotel in Boston demonstrated that he continued to be innovative with each design. Some improvements made in his 20 years of hotel building included construction of an attached office building and exterior light courts.

THE STATLER EMPIRE. Prior to his death in 1928, E.M. Statler built a total of seven hotels in six cities. Spread throughout New England and the Midwest, the members of this network enjoyed standard procedures and joint ad campaigns. Following Statler's death, the chain would continue to expand all the way to the Pacific.

THE BOAT TRIP. Several cities sought to become the site of Statler Hotel number three. By 1913, Statler narrowed his choices to either building new in Detroit or buying the William Penn in Pittsburgh. In a media stunt, Statler flipped a coin in front of several newsmen and announced he would make a boat trip to Detroit. He had failed to indicate what city each side of the coin represented beforehand. The Statler Company eventually leased the William Penn, 10 years after Statler's death.

THE JOHN J. BAGLEY HOUSE. When Statler stepped off of the boat, local booster Homer Warren enthusiastically greeted him. The two took a full Model T tour of the city, finally stopping at the intersection of Washington Boulevard and Grand Circus Park. There the old Italianate Villa of John J. Bagley stood amongst newer developments. Statler was impressed enough and decided to buy the site on the spot. (Burton Historical Collection.)

25

ARCHITECT'S PLANS. Shortly after securing the Bagley property, Statler put Post and Rorimer to work to build the best Statler yet. The site's triangular configuration would not prevent the designers from producing a worthy successor to the Cleveland house. First seen in this architect's rendering, the Detroit house was given an Italian Renaissance exterior that was influenced by Cleveland's but clearly unique. Of the structure's eighteen floors, the lower three were reserved for public spaces, the fourth for employee use, and the upper fourteen were divided into guest rooms. The plans on the following pages show the arrangement of these floors.

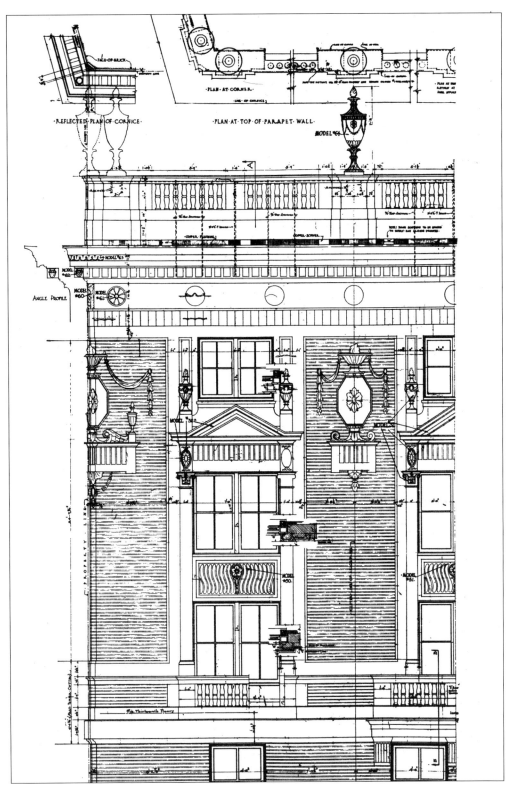

REFLECTED·PLAN·OF·CORNICE·

·PLAN·AT·CORNER·

PLAN·AT·TOP·OF·PARAPET·WALL·

MODEL ·64·

ANGLE·PROFILE·

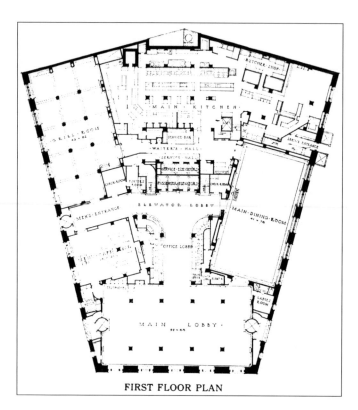

FIRST FLOOR PLAN

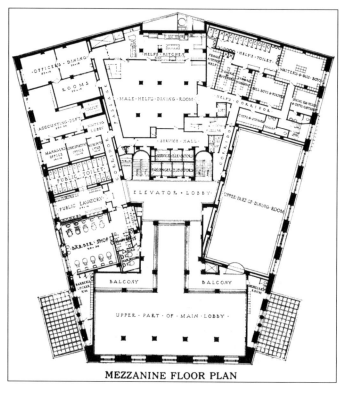

MEZZANINE FLOOR PLAN

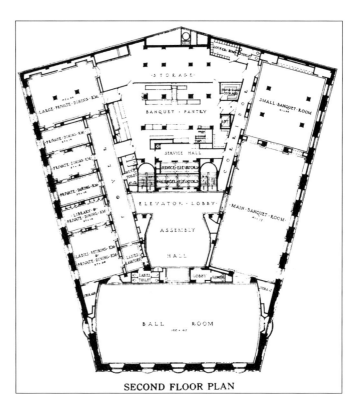

SECOND FLOOR PLAN

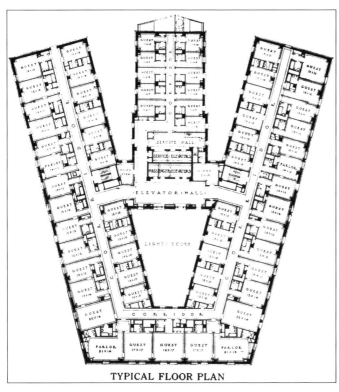

TYPICAL FLOOR PLAN

UNDER CONSTRUCTION. Construction would be rapid, taking only 18 months. Mayor Mark broke ground on August 1, 1913. Building the steel, concrete, and brick structure began on April 15, 1914, and was completed on August 15th. During the following months, workers installed Rorimer's grand interiors. Thus work continued right up to the day of the formal opening. The top photo shows the Statler fully framed and partly enclosed. In the lower photo, the exterior is complete. Construction of the Statler was matched by the Whitney Building and an extension of the Fuller Hotel.

A New Face on the Park. A sign over the Washington Boulevard entrance indicates that the Statler is not yet ready to open its 800 guest rooms in this early 1915 photograph. Additional construction at that time included the Tuller Hotel and the headquarters for the S.S. Kresge Company. (Burton Historical Collection.)

READY FOR BUSINESS. By February 1915, the new Statler was finally completed. Construction crews gave way to employees and decorators working at a feverous pace to prepare the hotel for its February 5 unveiling to the media. Finally, Detroiters were able to admire their newest hotel in all of its glory. On the evening of the fifth, 150 newsmen were given energetic tours of the hotel by Statler and his executives. The following day, the public read lengthy praises of the hotel's facilities and of Statler's "Rooseveltian Vim."

THE GRAND OPENING. On February 6, 1915, at 5:00 p.m., the new Statler Hotel officially opened for business. In a ceremony, Statler handed the keys of the hotel to its manager, Frederick B. Bergman. Two thousand Detroiters and five hundred guests from other cities were the lucky first guests. After a lavish dinner served in three settings in the Dining Room and Grill, the guests found dancing in the massive ballroom most enjoyable. And, thus, Detroit's first modern hotel was inaugurated to the music of two orchestras. (Walter P. Reuther Library, Wayne State University.)

THE WASHINGTON BOULEVARD ENTRANCE. This detail shot shows the main hotel entrance on Washington Boulevard. Each public entrance to the building sported a similar marquee to protect guests from the elements.

THE MAIN LOBBY. The most important public room on the ground floor was the lobby. Done in the Adam style, the room had a soft brown and gray-blue color scheme. The north wall had five arched windows facing a mezzanine balcony. Antiques Rorimer brought over from Europe were used to provide the space with tasteful furnishings.

THE OFFICE LOBBY. Identical in appearance to the main lobby, the office lobby led to the elevators and dining rooms. The offices were the heart of the hotel. Here one would find the registration offices and a newsstand. This space also provided access to the hotel's restaurants and four elevators. (Top: Matthew Furman.)

THE MAIN DINING ROOM. The Bagley Avenue side of the hotel was occupied by the large main dining room. This space continued the Italian and Adam style used throughout the hotel. With a Chinese-green color scheme, the room featured mirrors and wedge-wood panels. Service was top-rate. Male guests had to be in coat and tie in order to be seated. The soothing strains from the hotel's orchestra drifted down from the balcony. In later years, it was known as the Café Rouge.

DEPARTING FROM THE NORM. Two restaurants along Washington Boulevard departed from the Italian design, adapting an Elizabethan scheme. The Grill Room had brown oak walls and marble floors. The smaller Men's Café actually served as the hotel bar.

GRAND BALLROOM. Convention space figured prominently in the design of Statler Hotels. Thus, the entire third floor was given to that purpose. The largest room in the house was the Grand Ballroom. The Adam-styled room was colored in ivory and rose, the same colors used in all of the meeting rooms.

WAYNE ROOM. Just off of the ballroom, a second large banquet room was constructed. A removable wall allowed the two to be connected for larger functions. With its acoustical ceiling, the Wayne Room was one of the finest such rooms in the Statler organization.

LIBRARY. Among the smaller private meeting rooms that lined Washington Boulevard, one doubled as the hotel's library. Here guests could find reading material for the duration of their stay. Copies of *Statler Salesmanship*, the house magazine, were also kept in stock.

FOYER. This corridor ran the length of the Washington Boulevard side of the ballroom floor. The doors to the left lead to the hotel's small private dining rooms and the library. As additional meeting space was added, this corridor would be expanded.

THE LATEST LABOR SAVING DEVICES. E.M. Statler was always willing to provide the latest modern equipment, provided that it saved his employees their time and labor. Two such examples shown here are a modern dishwasher and a silver-buffing machine. Note the windows in the dishwashing room. Statler broke with tradition and placed his kitchens on the ground floor rather than the basement. This saved countless employee steps.

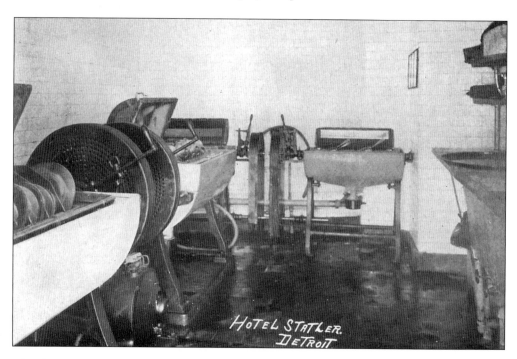

LIVING ROOM BY DAY. Even the smallest room in the Statler had to be comfortable. With the use of a Murphy Bed, this guest room could act as a living room by day and a bedroom at night. Later versions of this concept would use Studio Beds, beds that could be used as sofas during the day.

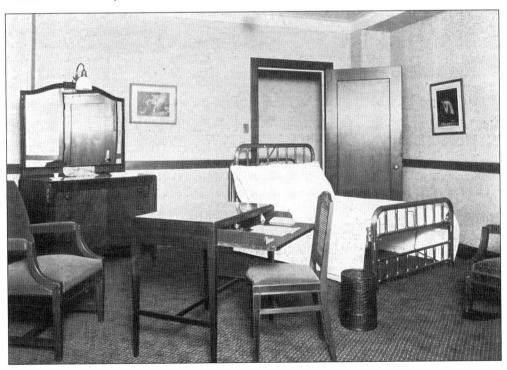

Schedule of Rates
Hotel Statler
Detroit

1000 Rooms   1000 Baths

Facing Grand Circus Park at Washington Boulevard and Bagley Avenue; convenient to all railroad terminals and steamer landings, with theater and shopping districts nearby.

Rooms with shower bath, for one $3.00 and $3.50; for two $5.00.

Rooms with tub and shower, for one $4.00, $4.50, $5.00 and up; for two $6.00, $6.50, $7.00 and up.

Rooms with twin beds (shower) $5.50; (tub and shower) $7.00 and up.

Parlor suites $13.00 and up. Private dining rooms and additional bedrooms (connecting) may be had if desired.

Sample rooms with bath, for one $5.00 and up; for two $7.00 and up.

PARLOR. In addition to the smaller rooms for businessmen and tourists, Statler provided luxury suites facing Grand Circus Park. Pictured here is the spacious parlor of one such suite.

THE GOOD OLD DAYS. One can't help but get nostalgic looking at this schedule of rates from 1923. The Statler offered a wide variety of rooms, but, regardless of room rate, every guest was ensured a private bath, circulating ice water, a free newspaper every morning, and the best Statler service.

EXPANSION. Statler's type of hotel proved to be just what Detroit wanted. Less than a year after opening, work had started on an addition along Washington Boulevard. Built by the Gray Estate Company, the new addition contained 200 guest rooms. The Statler could now advertise 1000 rooms and baths. The lower three floors of the addition housed retail space. (Burton Historical Collection.)

A Good Place to Get Sick. As new Statlers went up in other cities, new innovations went up with them. Whenever possible, these were incorporated into the older houses. One such example was the addition of an in-house medical department following the construction of the New York house. It included a clinic for guests. Hotel employees enjoyed an hour of service from 1–2 p.m. This photograph was taken from the east side of Grand Circus Park around 1917. The Book Building was still under construction. (From the Manning Brothers Historic Photographic Collection.)

Towering over Grand Circus Park. Automobiles still shared the road with horses at the time this photograph was taken during the First World War. However, the automobile is already clearly the preferred mode of transport.

Indoor Golf. To ensure that his hotels maintained Statler service, E.M. Statler enjoyed playing "indoor golf." In this process, he would stage surprise inspections to test the facilities and the employees. Once he disguised himself in the lobby and demanded an apple; he got the apple. For years, former Statler employees claimed that disaster was bound to strike whenever Statler was present. (Burton Historical Collection.)

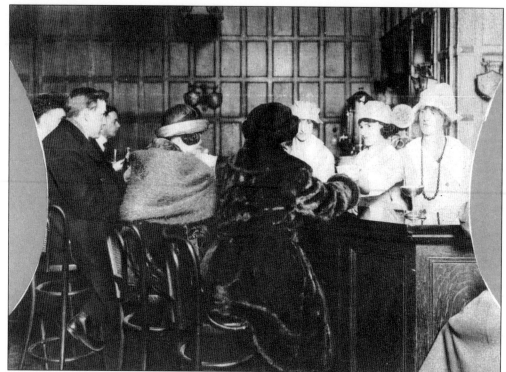

PROHIBITION. Most hotel men panicked when prohibition became the law of the land. The sale of alcohol had long been one of the industry's chief moneymakers. Statler saw no reason why these rooms couldn't continue to be profitable. He fitted them out as soda fountains and tearooms. Here we see the old Men's Café acting as a soda fountain. (Burton Historical Collection.)

TAKING A BREAK. This group of female Statlerites poses for a group shot on the roof in the mid-1920s. Their choice of the hotel's smoke stack for the background seems a bit odd. (Courtesy Nancy Bowman.)

POSTCARD ADVERTISING. Statler always sought ways to advertise the chain. It was only natural that he take advantage of the popularity of picture postcards and issue official company cards for his hotels. Bearing an image of the hotel on the front, they extolled the benefits of Statler service on the back.

A SECOND DETROIT STATLER? Apparently confident in the Detroit location, in 1923, E.M. Statler purchased land and had Post draw plans for a second 1,000 room Detroit hotel. Intended to rise over Woodward Avenue, this project was canceled at the last minute. (Burton Historical Collection.)

CONVENTIONS. A significant component of the Statler organization's business came from conventions. Thus, the Statler was designed to handle them. Here, a special welcome sign has been added to the Washington Boulevard marquee. Props, such as this tractor, could be lifted into the ballroom via a special hoist. (From the Manning Brothers Historic Photographic Collection.)

"EVERYONE SAY CHEESE!" Most conventions, large or small, hosted banquet dinners. This example from 1947 illustrates how the grand ballroom would be set up to accommodate several hundred diners. The ballroom could seat 600 in such fashion.

EXHIBITING THEIR PRODUCTS. Regardless of a group's size, the Statler kitchens could produce practically any meal desired. In this photograph from the early 1930s, Statler chefs have arranged a group of tempting desserts for the camera. By this time, most Statler cooking methods were scientifically standardized throughout the chain. This ensured a guest that his ice cream pie would be just as good in Detroit as it was in St. Louis. (Walter Reuther Library, Wayne State University.)

THE FOUNTAIN ROOM. By the time these 1935 photographs were taken, the old Men's Café still served as a place for guests to fill up with drinks like soda and tea. The room continued to retain much of its original design, but mirrors and bright paint had been added in an effort to liven up the space. (Both photos from the Manning Brothers Historic Photographic Collection.)

A MAKESHIFT BAR. With the end of Prohibition, the hotel industry was quick to return to the business of serving alcohol. This art deco bar was installed in the English Grill to serve the purpose. However, minor modifications such as this would not prove sufficient for long. (Manning Brothers Historic Photographic Collection.)

DARK TIMES. The dark areas above the hotel in this 1930s photograph symbolizes well the condition of the hotel industry during the Depression. Three of every four hotels went broke. Hotel building screeched to a halt. The Statler organization escaped financial disaster, though it had suffered the loss of its founder the year before the crash. (Manning Brothers Historic Photographic Collection.)

LOSING THE EDGE. As the 1930s wore on, the Statler organization began to lose its luster. The aging facilities began to show signs of wear and tear. Advertising slumped, and a lack of new construction projects virtually halted innovations. Morale was low among management and employees alike.

STATLERITES ON STRIKE. In 1937, Detroit experienced a number of strikes. The Statler was no exception. On March 16 of that year, the hotel employees effectively took over the hotel, throwing all of the guests out. A group of strikers were recorded occupying the dining room. (Walter Reuther Library, Wayne State University.)

THE TERRACE ROOM. Later that year, the hotel was dramatically remodeled in an effort to improve business. Louis Rorimer, the hotel's original decorator, oversaw the redecoration of the hotel's guest rooms and public spaces. The most notable change was the installation of a new restaurant complex in the former retail space of the 1916 addition. Done in a "modified Empire style," the Terrace Room was so named for its multiple levels of dining and dancing. The room was brilliantly colored in oyster white, ebony black, bluish green, and firecracker red. The Terrace Room was to serve as one of Detroit's primary nightspots for decades. Here people flocked to hear the likes of Desi Arnaz and Xavier Cugat. Few of the guests enjoying a luncheon seem to mind having their photo taken. (Manning Brothers Historic Photographic Collection.)

THE LOUNGE BAR. A companion to the Terrace Room, the Lounge Bar served alcohol in style. Open access to the Terrace Room allowed the music to be enjoyed while one sat at the bar. The keystone of the decor was a mural representing "The Age of the Vintner" by Paul Riba. Flesh-colored mirrors gave the effect that the room was larger than it was. The Terrace Room and Lounge Bar had their own entrance to Washington Boulevard. The old Grill and Men's Café were removed to provide space for a retail arcade connecting the new restaurants to the lobby. (Manning Brothers Historic Photographic Collection.)

THE CAFETERIA. In addition to glamorous high-class restaurants, a moderately priced self-serve cafeteria was carved out of the basement. Here, the budget or time-minded guest could grab a quick bite to eat prior to departing the hotel. Though inexpensive, the food was prepared in the same kitchens as the restaurants upstairs. The room was also air-conditioned. With air-conditioning added to all of the public areas, the Detroit Statler became the first American hotel to have the comforting convenience. (Manning Brothers Historic Photographic Collection.)

THE WASHINGTON BOULEVARD FAÇADE. This view from the early 1940s shows a typical scene along Washington Boulevard. However, the years of World War II were anything but typical. Much of the hotel's trained staff went off to war, putting a strain on service. Floods of travelers coming to Detroit on war business worsened the strain. From the darkness of the Great Depression, the Statler suddenly found itself with more guests than it could handle. (Manning Brothers Historic Photographic Collection.)

POSTWAR RECOVERY. By the end of the war, the Statler was much like it had been in early 1937, worn out. The high volume of traffic required considerable upgrades. Still, in this view from Grand Circus Park, the old hotel looks as beautiful and fresh as ever. By the end of the 1940s, the Statler Company's business reached new levels, and new construction projects promised continued prosperity. (Courtesy Nancy Bowman.)

THE HOTEL MANAGER. The manager of a hotel was an important figure in the community. Managers of the Statler would even be sought for advice and favors from prominent politicians. This photograph shows manager J.C. Meacham, who ran the hotel from 1945 to 1951. Statler managers were raised from within the company. Meacham previously managed the St. Louis house and would leave Detroit to manage the new Los Angeles Statler Center when it opened. (Courtesy Nancy Bowman.)

THE NEW TERRACE ROOM. After the war, the Terrace Room was completely redecorated from its "modified Empire style" into the space seen here. Despite the modified décor, it still offered the same popular music and dancing until its removal in 1963. (Courtesy Nancy Bowman.)

DOMINATING THE STREETSCAPE. The Statler seems to dominate the landscape in this late 1940s shot of pedestrians on Washington Boulevard. The Washington Theater is gone, and a clock sign has been added to the south end of the hotel. (Burton Historical Collection.)

THE BAGLEY ENTRANCE. In 1952, the old marquees were removed and replaced by modern glass block versions. This staged shot shows two businessmen in front of the Bagley Avenue entrance. (Burton Historical Collection.)

MODERN ELEVATORS. Throughout the late 1940s and 1950s, modifications slowly changed the classical appearance of the hotel. This photograph captures the new bank of elevators at the end of the office lobby. (Manning Brothers Historic Photographic Collection.)

THE END OF AN ERA. The hotel world changed on October 27, 1954. For a spectacular sum of $111 million, Conrad Hilton purchased the entire Statler organization. Thus, the Statler Hotels entered the largest hotel chain in the world. Despite claims that they would continue to maintain their unique features, by 1958, they were officially renamed Statler Hilton Hotels. However, the marquee had yet to be changed in this 1963 photograph of the Washington Boulevard entrance. (Walter P. Reuther Library, Wayne State University.)

TRADER VIC'S. Beginning in 1963, Hilton undertook a renovation program that replaced the Statler era restaurants with fresh ones. The most notable was the replacement of the Café Rouge with a Polynesian-themed restaurant named Trader Vic's. Serviced by its own entrance on Bagley, Trader Vic's is most remembered for its exotic drinks. (Top: Walter P. Reuther Library, Wayne State University.)

NEW MEETING SPACE. The reduction of the lobbies and dining room into single-story spaces created floor area for new meeting rooms. These rooms, actually a single large space, were named the Statler and Hilton rooms. Movable walls allowed them to be configured to a group's needs. (Burton Historical Collection.)

HOLDING UP QUITE WELL. The ballroom still presented an elegant appearance in the mid-1960s when this photograph was taken. The balconies were filled in and the fixtures replaced, but the room continued to maintain its charm. The unusual chandeliers date from post-war renovations. (Burton Historical Collection.)

IT'S THE DETROIT HILTON. Throughout the 1960s, the old Statler, as with most old downtown hotels, began to lose business. Newer hotels, roadside motels, and declining neighborhoods all shared the blame. Facing this sliding business, in 1969, Hilton sold the hotel to a group of 26 local investors known as the Detroit Hilton Limited Partnership for $7.2 million. Hilton would remain as the hotel's management, with a $6.2 million mortgage on the property, but no longer had the responsibility of ownership. This change of ownership was matched with a name change. The old Statler name was replaced with Detroit Hilton. This photo dates from 1974. (Walter P. Reuther Library, Wayne State University.)

THE DOORS CLOSE. Twenty years of Hilton management came to an end in 1974. The old Statler was renamed the Detroit Heritage Hotel. Unfortunately, business continued to slide for the new Heritage. By June 1975, hotel occupancy stood at a staggering 20 percent. This low business made it impossible for the hotel to pay all of its utility bills and taxes. On June 30, Detroit-Edison made its first threat to cut the hotel's steam and electrical service. Every effort was made to keep the Heritage open. First, Mayor Coleman Young and the local Teamsters Union sought a loan to keep the hotel in operation. By October, when this photograph was taken, the hotel's hopes rested within Pakistani financier Muhammad Farouk Kahn's plans to purchase the Heritage. Detroit-Edison held out until October 15. Sixty years after first opening its doors, E.M. Statler's great hotel was forced to close due to a lack of power or steam. (Walter P. Reuther Library, Wayne State University.)

Three
THE BOOK-CADILLAC HOTEL
1924–1984

THE TALLEST HOTEL IN THE WORLD. In 1924, the Statler Hotel finally found itself faced with a worthy rival. At the opposite end of Washington Boulevard, the Book brothers erected what was then the tallest hotel structure on earth. The Book-Cadillac offered all of the services and amenities that made the Statler famous. But the Book-Cadillac would become well known by its own right. Its dining rooms and nightclubs were nationally recognized. For almost 60 years, it would easily make any list of the finest hotels in the country. (Burton Historical Collection.)

LOUIS KAMPER. The architect the Book brothers choose to design their hotel had no previous experience with hotel design. Thus, Louis Kamper undertook an extensive study of American hotels. These included the Statler chain, the Willard in Washington, Chicago's Blackstone and La Salle, and the Copley-Plaza in Boston. Taking the best features from these noted hotels, Kamper set out to create the finest hotel in the country.

PLANNING A BIG HOTEL. All told, planning the Book-Cadillac required two years. Kamper decided to use the Italian Renaissance for decoration, much as George Post had done with the Statler. However, the Book-Cadillac would be decorated in a more elaborate Venetian manner. The massive hotel would have 29 floors, 3 basements, and 4 mechanical floors.

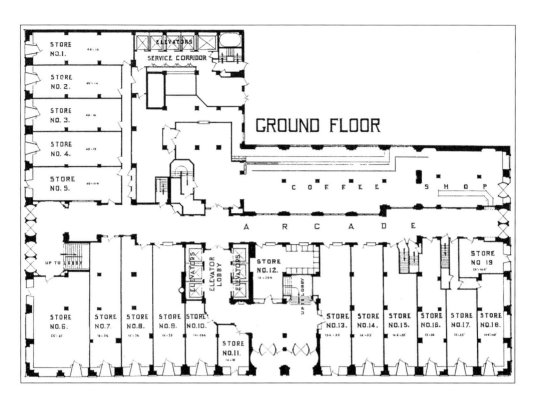

GROUND FLOOR

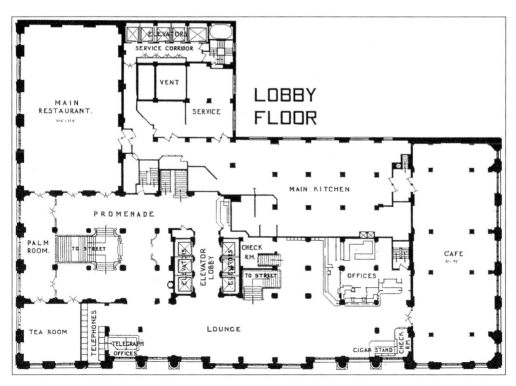

LOBBY FLOOR

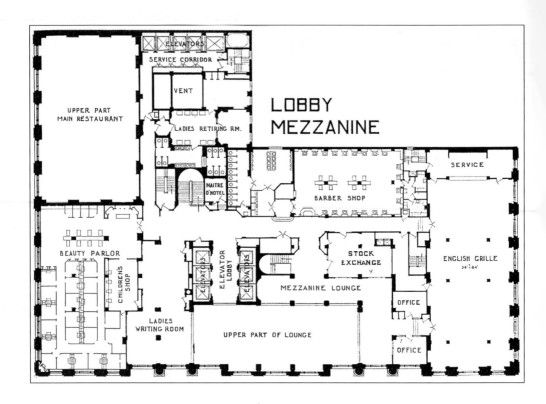

LOBBY MEZZANINE

UPPER PART MAIN RESTAURANT

ELEVATORS
SERVICE CORRIDOR
VENT
LADIES RETIRING RM.
MAITRE D'HOTEL
SERVICE
BARBER SHOP

BEAUTY PARLOR
CHILDREN'S SHOP
ELEVATORS
ELEVATOR LOBBY
ELEVATORS
STOCK EXCHANGE
ENGLISH GRILLE
MEZZANINE LOUNGE
OFFICE
LADIES WRITING ROOM
UPPER PART OF LOUNGE
OFFICE

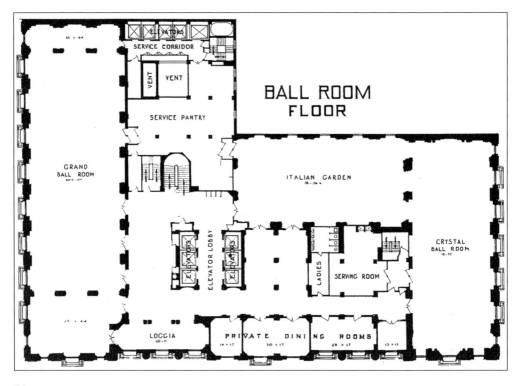

BALL ROOM FLOOR

ELEVATORS
SERVICE CORRIDOR
VENT VENT
SERVICE PANTRY

GRAND BALL ROOM

ITALIAN GARDEN

ELEVATORS
ELEVATOR LOBBY
ELEVATORS
LADIES
SERVING ROOM
CRYSTAL BALL ROOM

LOGGIA
PRIVATE DINING ROOMS

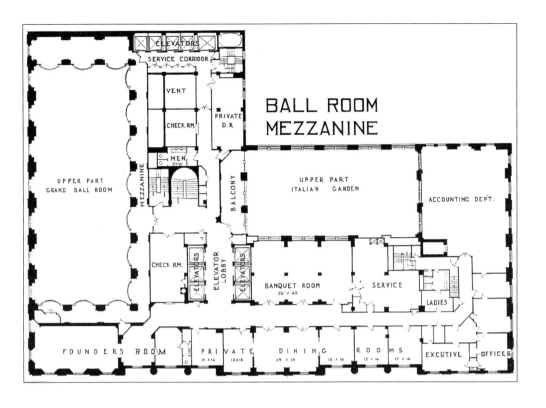

BALL ROOM
MEZZANINE

ELEVATORS

SERVICE CORRIDOR

VENT

CHECK RM.

PRIVATE D.R

MEN

UPPER PART
GRAND BALL ROOM

MEZZANINE

BALCONY

UPPER PART
ITALIAN GARDEN

ACCOUNTING DEPT.

CHECK RM.

ELEVATORS

ELEVATOR LOBBY

ELEVATORS

BANQUET ROOM
26' x 45

SERVICE

LADIES

FOUNDERS ROOM

PRIVATE DINING ROOMS
14 x 16   13 x 18   29 x 15   15 x 16   15 x 16   15 x 16

EXECUTIVE OFFICES

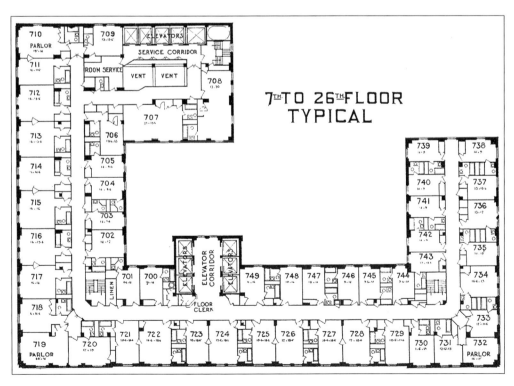

7TH TO 26TH FLOOR
TYPICAL

710 PARLOR

709

ELEVATORS

SERVICE CORRIDOR

711

ROOM SERVICE

VENT   VENT

708

712

707

713

706

705

704

714

703

715

702

716

701   700

LINEN

739

738

740

737

741

736

742

735

743

734

ELEVATORS   ELEVATOR CORRIDOR   ELEVATORS

717

FLOOR CLERK

749   748   747   746   745   744

733

718

719 PARLOR   720   721   722   723   724   725   726   727   728   729   730   731   732 PARLOR

EARLY INTERIOR STUDIES. The public would get its first glimpse of the Book-Cadillac's elegant interiors with these decorator studies. The top illustration shows the Venetian Dining Room much as it would appear when built. The lower illustration is of the Chinois Tea Room. As constructed, it would have a built-in bench lining the walls and carpeting on the floor.

THE BIG DIG. In order to provide space for three sub-basements and foundations, contractors had to remove over 60,000 cubic yards of dirt. By the time these photos were taken in September 1923, the hole was prepared for the placement of the foundations. Support of a 33-story skyscraper would require 20,000 barrels of cement, 600,000 pounds of structural steel, and over 8,800 cubic yards of concrete. (Both photos from the Manning Brothers Historic Photographic Collection.)

ALL FRAMED UP. The Book-Cadillac has assumed its familiar form in this remarkable photograph. Using an estimated 17,400,000 pounds of structural steel, the birdcage-like skeleton is nearly complete. Additional mind-boggling figures included 1,425,000 face bricks, 1,000,000 hollow bricks, 500,000 common bricks, and 850,000 sand lime bricks, which were required to enclose the structure. Decorative elements totaled 2,240 tons of building stone and 725 tons of terra cotta. These are fitting numbers for such an important building. (Manning Brothers Historic Photographic Collection.)

READY FOR BUSINESS. After two years of planning, construction, and the expense of over $16 million, the Book-Cadillac was ready for business by December 1924. In this photo, we see the completed hotel just prior to opening. For the first time, the full beauty if its unique façade and profile can be enjoyed. (Burton Historical Collection.)

THE GRAND OPENING GALA. As with the Statler, a gala grand opening was staged. On the evening of December 8, 1924, over 2,000 guests descended upon the hotel. Every room was filled to capacity, and over 3,000 people were turned away. The public rooms were filled to capacity for the opening dinner. The Book family dined at a table in the Venetian Dining Room situated in the same spot they had dined in the old Cadillac Hotel's dining room.

MICHIGAN AVENUE FAÇADE. Detroit was more than impressed with their newest hotel. The local papers devoted large spreads to its accolades. The national industry magazine *Hotel Bulletin* published a special volume devoted solely to describing its wonders. In this mid-1920s photograph, we get a glimpse of the impressive Michigan Avenue façade. This view is now blocked by additional buildings. (Burton Historical Collection.)

FROM THE BOOK BUILDING. In addition to being a physically impressive building itself, the Book-Cadillac's massive size instantly became a key feature of Washington Boulevard. This shot, taken from the Book Building at a rarely photographed angle, reveals how the building appeared along the Boulevard. (Manning Brothers Historic Photographic Collection.)

ROOF-TOP RADIO. Not only was the Book-Cadillac the tallest hotel in the world, it was the tallest building in the city in 1924. Thus, its penthouse was the ideal home for the WCX broadcasting station. Massive antennas installed for this purpose dominate the view shown here. (Burton Historical Collection.)

A CROWNED JEWEL. Standing proud in the city skyline, the Book-Cadillac's unique roofline gave the impression that the building wore a crown. This image was printed in the Detroit News. (Burton Historical Collection.)

REACHING FOR THE TOP. Twenty-nine floors over Washington Boulevard, a gutsy Detroit Free Press painter strikes a dramatic pose on one of the copper terraces that figure prominently in the hotel's exterior. (Burton Historical Collection.)

THE PROMENADE. Guests entered the hotel via a staircase of Breche Violette marble that led up to this Italian lounge. Here, one could relax in a sea of gray-green carpeting with the bustling lobby just around the corner.

THE MAIN LOBBY. The Venetian Main Lobby typified the attention to detail Kamper put into his hotel. The walls were imported Breche Violette marble. The plaster ceiling, emblazoned with the Cadillac coat-of-arms, was covered in gold leaf. A balcony of wrought iron and walnut surrounded three sides of the lobby space. Surrounded by these elegant features were the registration desk, a telegraph office, and a cigar stand.

THE VENETIAN DINING ROOM. No other room in the hotel symbolized the grandeur of the Book-Cadillac than its Venetian Dining Room. The vaulted ceiling was covered in murals. The green walls of exotic carved woods featured massive paintings representing the seasons. Bronze chandeliers and red carpeting completed the effect. The room was so overwhelming that it's a wonder anyone could pay attention to the food. But it was here that some of the city's best food was served.

THE BLUE ROOM CAFÉ. French in design, this large restaurant served as an alternative to the Venetian Dining Room. Its walls were of walnut, enhanced by blue and gold draperies. In recognition of the need for dance, the central portion of carpeting could be removed for an evening of entertainment.

THE PALM ROOM. It was the after-dinner crowd that Kamper had in mind when he designed the Palm Room. Guests could enjoy their coffee or tea amongst light green and ivory furnishings. The brightly colored ceiling featured the initials "BC."

THE COFFEE SHOP. As the Statler would with its cafeteria, the Book-Cadillac provided a moderately priced self-serve restaurant for its guests. The Coffee Shop was the only public area on the ground floor. The room was simple in design compared to its upstairs rivals. Walls were cream, with blue and gold accents.

A MALE DOMAIN. Reserved solely for the use of male patrons, the English Grille on the Mezzanine was a low-beamed English affair. The oak-walled room was designed to resemble a club. Completing the effect was a service of specially designed china featuring English hunting scenes. An innovative feature was an elaborate display case (below) from which guests could select their meats.

THE GRAND BALLROOM. If the Book-Cadillac were to truly rival the Statler, it would need a large collection of convention space. Thus, its Grand Ballroom was built with a slightly larger floor area than that of the Statler's. The Florentine room featured two chandeliers with over a ton of crystal each. Innovative radio broadcasting and amplifying equipment was one of its notable technological features.

THE CRYSTAL BALLROOM. The Crystal Ballroom, so named for its light fixtures, took up the opposite end of the ballroom floor. The mirrored walls were highlighted with white, gold, and ivory highlights. Like the grand ballroom, it also featured radio equipment.

A Little Piece of Italy. As beautiful as the Grand and Crystal Ballrooms were, the Italian Garden was unquestionably the most striking of the Book-Cadillac's three ballrooms. The room was intended to give visitors the sense that they were standing in the garden of an Italian villa. The walls were covered with vegetation. An incredible glass ceiling played a key role in achieving the desired effects. Employing special light and sound devices, this ceiling could replicate virtually any type of weather. One minute it could be a sunny day, then simulated dark clouds would roll in and a thunderstorm began. After a while, the storm would pass and it would be a beautiful cloudless night.

LOGGIA. This spacious loggia served as a foyer for the three main ballrooms. Designed in a Louis XV theme, the room had rose carpeting and furniture from Sarah Bernhardt's drawing room.

WOMEN'S RETIRING ROOMS. If women guests couldn't use the English Grille, they could use the series of retiring rooms reserved for their use. This complex contained a powder room, rest room, and smoking room.

BEAUTY PARLOR.
Suspiciously close to
the Women's Retiring
Rooms sat the Beauty
Parlor. The Louis XIV
space also had the
advantage of an
adjacent children's play
room.

**THE BARBER
SHOP.** The
hotel's barber
shop was called
"the most
complete and
attractive thing
of its kind in
America." Even
if the statement
was an
exaggeration,
the green tiled
space was an
equal with the
other public
areas of the
hotel.

LOBBY FURNITURE. The entire task of equipping and furnishing the Book-Cadillac was given to the Albert Pick Company of Chicago. It was the single largest such job ever. Despite its size, the Albert Pick workers performed their duties most skillfully. This selection of furniture was chosen to occupy the lobby. Many of the pieces were antiques.

MODERN KITCHENS. One of the most significant differences between the Book-Cadillac and the Statler was the arrangement of their kitchens. The Statler was built around its kitchens, so that all of the kitchens were arranged on top of each other and connected via service elevators. The Book-Cadillac's were more spread out, as the English Grille and Coffee Shop were provided with their own separate units. Still, the Book-Cadillac was equipped with the latest equipment, such as these gas ranges.

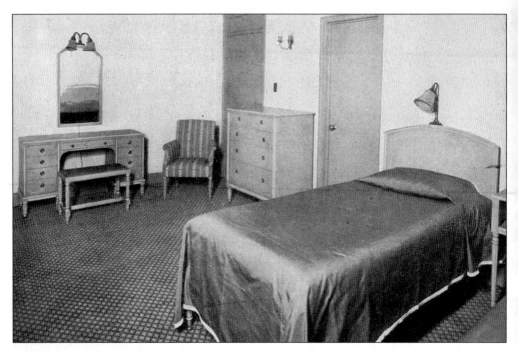

THE HEART OF THE HOTEL. For all their grandeur, the public areas of a hotel were just icing on the cake. The true heart of the Book-Cadillac were the 1,136 guest rooms spread throughout the seventh through twenty-ninth floors. Although bare by today's standards, these rooms were top-notch in 1924. As with the Statler, every room — from the luxury suites to the smallest single — had a private bath.

SOMETHING'S AFOOT. A massive crowd has gathered at the Washington Boulevard entrance in this undated photo. The look of the crowd does not suggest that a convention is in the house. A major social event or the arrival of a celebrity are more likely possibilities. Over the years, the Book-Cadillac hosted the likes of Presidents Truman, Eisenhower, Kennedy, Johnson, and Nixon, as well as Eleanor Roosevelt and Errol Flynn. Although no identification accompanies this photo, it does illustrate the traffic that hotels could bring to the Boulevard. (Manning Brothers Historic Photographic Collection.)

DON'T KNOW HOW TO GET THERE? Just in case one didn't know the way to Detroit, the publishers of this postcard provided a nice map in addition to a photo of the hotel. This postcard dates from the 1930s. By then, the Book brothers had lost control of their proud hotel in the wake of the Great Depression.

ENGLISH ROOM BAR. Society was changing, and the English Grille's days as a male-only club did not last long. It was later used as a bar, before the construction of a proper cocktail lounge. For most of its life, the English Room served as an additional meeting room. (Manning Brothers Historic Photographic Collection.)

ONE ROOM, MANY USES. The large, column-free expanses of the Book-Cadillac's meeting rooms made it possible to use them for a number of functions. In the top photo, we see the Crystal Ballroom set up with displays awaiting a flood of conventioneers. Below is the same room for a presentation at a convention. The Crystal Ballroom could accommodate 500 people in such a meeting setup. The room's wooden floor and proximity to a kitchen also made it a site of dances and banquets. (Both photos from the Manning Brothers Historic Photographic Collection.)

ALL SET FOR THE SHOW. As with the Crystal Ballroom, the Grand Ballroom could accommodate a wide range of activities. This photograph shows the room set up with exhibitor's displays. The room's built-in lighting must not be doing the trick. A network of extra lights has been hung from the balcony. (Manning Brothers Historic Photographic Collection.)

JUST A LITTLE GAME OF BRIDGE. The Grand Ballroom appears to be filled to the brim in this 1941 photo of the Union Guardian bridge party. This unusual photograph further illustrates the wide range of activities the hotel's ballrooms could accommodate. Note that the balconies are also in use. (Walter P. Reuther Library, Wayne State University.)

Enjoying a Talk in the English Room. Something in the faces of these individuals indicates that they may not be thoroughly entertained by the talk they are attending. This photograph reveals the former English Grille functioning as a meeting room. Few alterations have been made. (Manning Brothers Historic Photographic Collection.)

GENERAL MOTORS FLEET SALES
BOOK-CADILLAC HOTEL, DETROIT
WEDNESDAY, DECEMBER 13, 1933.

A Private Party. If a group wasn't large enough to warrant use of one of the ballrooms for their function, the Book-Cadillac had a range of smaller meeting rooms to offer. This room adjoined the Grand Ballroom in the event the larger facility needed further space.

WASHINGTON BOULEVARD IN THE 1930S. In 1931, the effects of the Great Depression forced the Book-Cadillac into receivership. With that, the Books lost their prized hotel. The Book-Cadillac soon fell under the wing of hotelman Ralph Hitz's National Hotel Management Company. Now part of a national network of hotels, the Book-Cadillac was now operated on Hitz's well-known policies on service. Management would be known to ask a guest if everything was alright, be it their room or the weather. By contrast, the Statler operated on a policy that if something was wrong, then the guest would let you know. (Burton Historical Collection.)

THE BOOK-CASINO. When the Statler opened its new Terrace Room in 1937, the Book-Cadillac would not be outdone. The old Venetian Dining Room, a room that had included so much craftsmanship, was completely removed. In its place went the Book-Casino. Amid smooth woods and glass blocks, diners would enjoy dancing to the sounds of Joe Reichman or Del Delbridge. The Book-Casino was a worthy rival to the Terrace Room.

THE ESQUIRE ROOM. In addition to the removal of the Venetian Dining Room for the Book-Casino, the Esquire Room replaced the old Blue Room Café. The richly carved walnut gave way for smooth wood surfaces, while the elaborate French ceiling was covered. The room continued in its old function. It was a dining alternative to the Book-Casino, with occasional dancing. (Manning Brothers Historic Photographic Collection.)

GUEST ROOM. Remodeling went beyond public areas. Guest rooms were the most important part of the hotel, and every attempt was made to make them up-to-date and attractive. In this room, the register has been mocked up to resemble a bookcase.

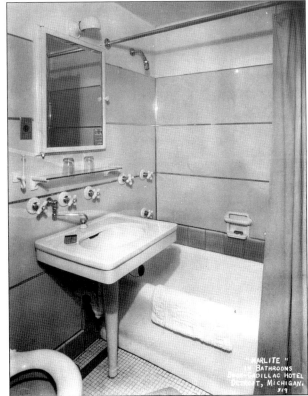

REMODELED BATHS. Even the bathrooms were subject to modernization. This Book-Cadillac restroom has been spruced up with a covering of Marlite over the original tile. Note the specially made bathmat.

WELCOMING A CONVENTION. Washington Boulevard was crowded when this picture was taken in the late 1940s. A series of futuristic-looking charter buses, likely in use for a convention, are parked in front of the Washington Boulevard entrance. A welcome sign offers the convention a big hello. A large sign added to the marquee advertises who will be performing in the Book-Casino and Motor Barn. (Burton Historical Collection.)

Enter the Sheraton Corporation. Twenty years after the Book brothers lost control of their hotel, it sold again. The large hotel chains were expanding more with acquisition than new construction, and, in 1951, the Sheraton Corporation chose the Book-Cadillac as its Detroit location. Reportedly, Sheraton paid six million dollars for 70 percent of the hotel's stock. The most obvious effect of this change of ownership was the new name Sheraton-Cadillac. We see the new name here on a modern Washington Boulevard marquee. (Burton Historical Collection.)

Detroit's

SHERATON-CADILLAC HOTEL

1114 WASHINGTON BOULEVARD
DETROIT 31, MICHIGAN WOODWARD 1-8000

A TOP MONEYMAKER. The purchase of the Book-Cadillac proved to be a wise investment for Sheraton. Throughout the 1950s and 1960s, the hotel was a top moneymaker for the company. With advertisements and promotional literature, the company went to lengths to inform the public of the name change and that the hotel's famed service would go unchanged. To increase the hotel's appeal, Sheraton would also undertake a series of interior and exterior physical renovations.

CAFÉ CAPRICE. By the 1960s, what had been the Chinois Tearoom had been transformed through several renovations into the Café Caprice. It maintained its basic function as a watering hole, though the room's décor had little in common with its original design. A built-in television testifies to the type of preferred entertainment. (Courtesy Matthew Furman.)

A GRAND ESCALATOR. In the postwar world, modern conveniences such as escalators were valued more than features with architectural grandeur such as the grand staircase of Breche Violette marble. In this scene, a bellboy in a futuristic uniform is evidently aiding a departing guest.

THE MOTOR BAR. The Motor Bar was a popular dining room on the ground floor, facing Washington Boulevard. Appropriately named, the Motor Bar boasted a mural of antique automobiles. The room actually dated from the 1930s, when it was known as the Café Cadillac.

THE 1960S. The Sheraton-Cadillac continued to be a popular hotel for visitors and Detroiters alike. However, as the 1960s wore on, business began to slip. As with the Statler, the Sheraton-Cadillac found itself with new competition and a changing neighborhood. Note the absence of the exterior cornice. It was removed around 1960. (Burton Historical Collection.)

104

Ho Ho Ho! Throughout its history, the hotel celebrated the holidays in style. This photograph from the mid-1960s shows the types of elaborate displays that were erected inside and out of the building. Taking time to enjoy the holiday decorations at the big downtown hotels became a tradition. (Burton Historical Collection.)

THE WHAT-CADILLAC? The hotel would have four names in the five years between 1975 and 1980. Due to slumping business, in 1975, Sheraton sold the hotel to Herbert Weissberg. Renamed the Detroit-Cadillac, within a year Weissberg lost the hotel, and it became the Radisson-Cadillac. By 1979, Radisson was dumped, and the hotel was renamed Book-Cadillac. The shoddy sign reflects the constant name changes. (Walter P. Reuther Library, Wayne State University.)

DRESSED UP FOR THE REPUBLICAN NATIONAL CONVENTION. The 1980 Republican National Convention briefly saved the Book-Cadillac. The Detroit Economic Growth Corporation staved off an announced closing in 1979. The hotel was refurbished in hopes that it could be revived. Following the convention, plans were drawn up to convert the building into a luxury hotel with offices. The Book-Cadillac closed in November 1984 for renovations. When the developers backed out, it did not reopen. (Burton Historical Collection.)

Four
THE HOTELS TODAY

THE PEOPLE MOVER. Twenty-seven years since its closing, the Statler still presents a proud appearance to Grand Circus Park. This photograph catches a People Mover train as it travels around the hotel. Some sources claim that the amount of money spent over the downtown transit system's budget could have renovated the Statler three times. The line of windows filled with plywood is evidence of a state-funded site clean-up completed in early 2002.

THE BOULEVARD SIDE. Visible along the upper portions of the façade, it appears that netting has been added to prevent brick or other pieces of the building from falling to the street. The downside to the addition of the People Mover is its close proximity to the building, passing within feet of the Ballroom.

WASHINGTON BOULEVARD ENTRANCE. The details of the Statler's entrance are weathered but still show their classic beauty. Faded awnings and panels date from December 1988, when they were installed to improve the view from People Mover trains.

THE EFFECTS OF WATER INFILTRATION. Lack of roof maintenance has resulted in water infiltration throughout the building. The result is an accelerated deterioration of the interiors. This room is the Beef Barron restaurant, installed in 1963 in the former Terrace Room. (Courtesy Dan Kosmowski.)

SILENT CORRIDORS. Once filled with guests and hotel employees, the various corridors of the Statler sit in eerie silence. As with the Beef Barron, they display signs of water damage. Both wallpaper and plaster are falling off the walls. (Bottom: Dan Kosmowski.)

EVERY ROOM WITH A VIEW. To allow every guest room a window, a light court was installed in the center of the Statler. It is said that when this space was being constructed, E.M. Statler noticed, with his naked eye, a group of windows being built out of line.

STATLER GUEST ROOM. The typical guest room today has been cleared of all its furnishings. This room on the sixth floor is in good condition but littered with debris. How many different people slept here? If only walls could talk.

THE GRAND BALLROOM. Of all of the Statler's original public rooms, the ballroom is the most recognizable. The massive space is largely intact, save one corner where an open window has allowed further deterioration. Once a center of activity, only the sound of passing People Mover trains breaks the silence. (Courtesy Dan Kosmowski.)

THE LAST GUEST. Unfortunately, even though the hotel is closed, there are individuals who have needed to seek shelter here. It is unlikely that the individual who arranged this apartment knew he was in part of the manager's private quarters. (Courtesy Dan Kosmowski.)

THE STATLER SHAFT. In its decayed state, sections of the hotel reveal how they were put together. This medicine cabinet has opened to show the Statler plumbing shaft, which allowed the presence of a private bathroom with every guest room.

DAMAGE OF A DIFFERENT SORT. Not all damage to the Statler is the result of natural decay. The scrap metal content of the building's systems, as well as architectural artifacts, have attracted vandals who open up walls and shafts to loot the building.

SOLD, SOLD, DETROIT-CADILLAC. However, most of the items removed from the Statler were done so at the liquidation sale in 1976. The scrawling on this door indicates that the contents of the room were all sold to the Detroit-Cadillac, as the Book-Cadillac was then known. Later, it was argued that the hotel had been so plundered at the sale that it was cost prohibitive to re-equip and repair it.

THE BOOK-CADILLAC. The roof of the Statler provides a fine view of Washington Boulevard and the Book-Cadillac Hotel. By the 1990s, most of the street's historic buildings remained in place. (Courtesy Dan Kosmowski.)

THE BOOK-CADILLAC LIGHT COURT. Like the Statler, the Book-Cadillac was built with a light court. However, its court faced an alley. This allowed the hotel to advertise itself as having all "outside" rooms. This view was taken from the roof of the David Stott Building. (Courtesy Dan Kosmowski.)

A NUMBER OF IDEAS. Since its closing, there have been several attempts to reopen the Book-Cadillac. Efforts to make the Book-Cadillac Plaza hotel/office complex a reality continued until 1986. Since the 1990s, there have been rumors of its use as a luxury hotel and casino. A 2002 feasibility study by the Detroit Economic Growth Corporation has made an upcoming redevelopment of the site more likely.

FOUR GUARDIANS. Perhaps the Book-Cadillac's most interesting exterior feature are these four statues built over the Michigan Avenue entrance. They are all characters connected to the early history of Detroit. From left to right they are General Anthony Wayne, Antoine De La Mothe Cadillac, Pontiac, leader of Pontiac's Rebellion, and Navarre, Cadillac's lieutenant. (Courtesy Dan Kosmowski.)

MICHIGAN AVENUE FAÇADE. The longest of the hotel's façades, the Michigan Avenue face looms high over the street.

WASHINGTON BOULEVARD FAÇADE. Vacant for 18 years, the hotel shows signs of wear in this 2002 shot. The entrances are blocked and awnings tattered. However, the exterior is still impressive.

ENGLISH GRILLE. Like the Statler, the Book-Cadillac has suffered from water infiltration. Unaltered by renovations, the English Grille has deteriorated severely. Much of the wood paneling has peeled off. (Courtesy Dan Kosmowski.)

CRYSTAL BALLROOM. Located one floor above the English Grille, the Crystal Ballroom has also suffered much of the same water damage. (Courtesy Dan Kosmowski.)

BEFORE MINING. As with the Statler, the Book-Cadillac has been mined of scrap metals and architectural ornaments. However, prior to 1997, a guard kept the miners away. Seen in this view of the ballroom, the chandeliers remain in place. (Courtesy Dan Kosmowski.)

FOLLOWING THE MINING. With the removal of the guard, miners wasted no time ridding the hotel of its remaining ornamental metals. This 2000 photograph shows the same ballroom but without the chandeliers. Pieces of those fixtures have been found in antique stores around metro Detroit. (Courtesy Dan Kosmowski.)

SURVIVORS. There are portions of the hotel's interior ornaments that have remained out of reach of a miner's ladder. Such is the case of this decorative head in the Grand Ballroom.

EMPTY CORRIDOR. Like the Statler, the Book-Cadillac's corridors are eerily dark and quiet. Some floors were closed before the hotel closed. The result is a mix of decorating schemes throughout the hotel. This corridor is in the decorative scheme used in the hotel's last renovation.

A ROOM WITH A VIEW. The Book-Cadillac's great height makes it a superb platform for views of Washington Boulevard. From here, the Statler is made to look almost puny. (Courtesy Dan Kosmowski.)

BROADCASTING PENTHOUSE. High above the Book-Cadillac's guest rooms, the empty ruin of the old WCX broadcasting studio remains intact. The radio equipment is long gone. The presence of a bed in one room suggests its later use as an apartment. (Courtesy Dan Kosmowski.)

THE MICHIGAN AVENUE FAÇADE. The roof of the Lafayette Building, another Kamper design, makes a splendid platform for viewing the Michigan Avenue and Shelby Street corner of the hotel. (Courtesy Dan Kosmowski.)

AN UNCERTAIN FUTURE. Even though it hasn't accepted a guest since 1984, the Book-Cadillac remains an impressive monument to its era and the three brothers that dreamt of a greater Washington Boulevard. We see it here towering over Shelby Street like a soaring mountain. Both the Book-Cadillac and Statler are important physical features of their respective landscapes. The destruction of either one would be a tragedy.

AFTERWORD

At the time I am writing this, both the Statler and Book-Cadillac are still standing but face uncertain futures. With the failure of a 1999 Request For Proposal on the Statler, demolition seems almost certain. Unfortunately, the current economic climate is a roadblock in getting the numbers to favor its renovation.

The Book-Cadillac's situation is more hopeful, yet still uncertain. The Detroit Economic Growth Corporation is conducting feasibility studies to determine what it would take to bring the building back. A group of concerned citizens have formed The Friends of the Book-Cadillac Hotel, hoping to encourage renovation. Meanwhile, developers and hotel chains have expressed interest in the building. But whether the numbers will work remains to be seen. It would not be the first time a proposal for the hotel has fallen through.

What is certain is that the hotels have sat empty for far too long. Should they reopen, they will again become valuable economic and social gems to the city.

David Kohrman
July 2002

BIBLIOGRAPHY

English, Carey. "City Gets Heritage for Unpaid Taxes." *Detroit Free Press*. 26 June, 1979: 3A.

Ferry, W. Hawkins. *The Buildings of Detroit: A History*. Detroit: Wayne State University Press, 1980.

Fogel, Helen. "Radisson Cadillac Opens its Doors." *Detroit Free Press*. 24 April, 1978: 4D.

The Hotel Bulletin Describing The Book-Cadillac. Chicago: Ben. P. Branham Company, 1925.

"Hotel Statler, Detroit, Mich." *Architecture and Building*. March 1915: 89–101.

"How the Book-Cadillac Will be Operated." *The Detroiter*. December 1924: 11–13.

Jarman, Rufus. *A Bed for the Night: The Story of E.M. Statler and His Remarkable Hotels*. New York: Harper & Brothers,1952.

Jay, Leah. "Remember When it Was 'The Book'." *Sunday News Magazine* 8 December 1974.

Kosmowski, Dan. May 1999. The Book-Cadillac I've Known. 15 July, 2002 http://www.dkpdetroit.com/bc/.

"Landmark Hotel Renovation Slated." *Detroit Monitor*. 18 Jan., 1978: 1+.

Lee, Richard. "Grand Circus Park Getting a Tune-Up for Big Auto Show." *Detroit Free Press*. 22 Dec., 1988: 1A.

Miller, Floyd. *Statler: America's Extraordinary Hotelman*. New York: The Statler Foundation, 1968.

"New Rooms at Detroit-Cleveland Statlers." *Mid-West Hotel Reporter*. Jan., 1938: 5.

Ratliff, Rick. "Ghost Hotels—A New Life?" *Detroit Free Press*. 6 Feb, 1983: 1B.

Tempest, Rone. "It Wasn't the Plaza or Ritz, But it Was Detroit's Best." *Detroit Free Press*. 9 Oct.. 1975: A3.